Daddy!

Letters to Discovery

TIFFANY DAWN BURCH

BLUEPRINT PRESS
INTERNATIONALE

Daddy!
Copyright © 2022 by Tiffany Dawn Burch

ISBN
978-1-959365-13-6 (Paperback)
978-1-959365-14-3 (eBook)
978-1-959365-12-9 (Hardcover)

Table of Contents

Acknowledgment

There are so many lives which have helped weave the threads for this book to be put together. First and foremost, I must give glory to God! He not only gave me the gift of writing, He connected me with key people to develop my voice and channel my emotions. Without God, this book would not be.

Next, I must give credit to my daddy who always inspired and encouraged me to live out the dreams God wrote on my heart. Likewise, my mom was the one who introduced me to the joy of writing even as young as five. She never let our social status or preconceived notions define who we were. I was taught to explore my creative side while diving into intelligence at a young age. To my mom: Thank you, Mom, for not seeing me as ordinary and for showing me that I can be extraordinary. Also, thank you for letting me share your very intimate letter to Dad; your words will touch the hearts of many. I love and appreciate all you sacrificed for Dad and your children.

Additionally, I have to recognize the ones who I grew up with, the ones who challenged me and pushed me to be the best I could in everything I did. First, I must say a thank you to my sister, Patty, who showed me that despite what the world says, you can rise above it. Patty, thank you for being a listening ear, for being a sound board for my creative vision for this book, and for contributing your journal entries to show another voice of this grief. You are my little hero, and I am so excited how God is going to use you in the future.

To my brothers, Mitch, Jerry, and Tim, this book is for you. Brothers, you are so important to me! You all taught me how to fight and survive. Thank you; let these words minister to your heart as you conquer your grief. I love all three of you, no matter what!

Along the way God put many wonderful teachers and principals in my path. I have to give thanks to Neosho Heights School and Mr. Harris from

Oswego, Kansas. It was because of them that my desire to write began to be nurtured and encouraged. These were the building blocks I needed to lay down the foundation for my future as a writer.

For me there was a defining moment that would change the course I would travel as a writer forever. This would be December of my seventh grade year when I met face-to- face the woman who would be the greatest mentor I would ever have as a writer, Mrs. Jaime Stephens. However, this relationship started off bittersweet. By this time, I knew I was a gifted writer. Imagine the shock I experienced when I received my first red-marked (bloodied) paper. I cried, but this moment humbled my young heart. The fundamental skills I learned from Mrs. Stephens would take me beyond my years as a young writer. To Mrs. Stephens: Thank you for being a friend when I had none, for encouraging me, for listening to me, and for all the extra hours you let me stay after school to play on the computers. Thank you for helping me discover and develop my voice. I will never forget you!

Likewise, I have to acknowledge Miami First Assembly of God in Miami, Oklahoma, who gave me a platform to share my poetry as a young teenager. To the people of that church who have prayed for me and with me, who have taught me and encouraged me, who have loved me, I say, thank you all for your prayers; thank you for all who taught me! I love you all.

In the same way I have to say thank you to NEO Christian Student Ministry who also gave me a platform to read my poetry: Thank you for all you did to try to steer me on the right path! I will never forget what you did for me. I love you all!

To the University of Oklahoma Chi Alpha Ministries, I must acknowledge Pastor Greg and Susan Tiffany, State Chi Alpha Directors, Pastor Nick; Blake; Jackie; Edie; Erin; Cassie; Megan; McKinzie; and so many more who helped me in ways they cannot even imagine. They showed me how to open my heart again and receive the love of God. I say to them, thank you for loving me, despite me. Thank you for reaching out to me, especially the moments when my daddy died. God used each of you in huge ways in my life, and I will never forget your kindness, your encouragement, your friendship, and your love. I pray God bless each and every one of you in all you do!

This leads me to the final chapter of this book. I must acknowledge New Beginnings Church in McAlester, Oklahoma. This family of God gave me a home to belong and to grow more and more in the Word of God. Pastor Kenny and Sister Rachel Springer, Brother Frank and Sister Jenneffer Parker, Sister Audrey Foshee, and so many others have poured their love into me. Thank you all for your patience, your encouragement, your prayer, and for adhering to the Word of God. It is because of all you have instilled in me through God that I finished this book. I love each and every one of you. I am thankful God brought me to you all and that I am able to be a part of your family.

Finally, I have to say thank you to the Regina Project; it led me to this victory! The Regina Project, a women's ministry for life after crisis, opened its arms wide and embraced me as I was. Pastor Randy and Glenda, I love you two like my parents! You have given me more than you can imagine. Thank you for being by my side in the good and the bad and never giving up on me. Thank you for showing me to walk in success and that I am a queen in God's eyes. I love you both, and I look forward to writing my next book about how the ministry changed my life!

To Sister Lonna Watkins of the Regina Project, thank you for letting me shadow you even when it looked like I was never going to come out to the other side and for allowing God to show up and show off in my life. I love and appreciate you so much!

To all my Regina Project Sisters: Thank you for loving me, for showing me what it means to be a friend, for teaching me how to be a woman of God, and helping me get to the other side of my grief! Also, to all of you sisters who agreed with me in prayer for this book to come to pass, thank you! God used your prayers to seal the desire and faith I had in my heart. You must know I love each and every one of you, and know that if God did it for me, He can do it for you!

Preface

July 8, 2009
Dear reader:

I am writing you today to tell you never give up on your dreams: you have a purpose, and God always wins! Those two ingredients alone will take you farther than you could ever know. I am Tiffany, or Tif as what friends call me and for whatever reason, you have picked this book up, so let me lead you through my grief; know this is only the beginning...

If it is grief that led you here, I don't know you, but I feel your pain. So trust me when I say you can get through this. I know you can!

If it is curiosity, let that eagerness take you into the minds of your friends who are hurt beyond words they can even speak.

I trust God that whatever your reason is, you will use this ammunition in your fight against a silent killer: grief!

Yours truly,

Tif
Tiffany Dawn Burch

Daddy to Me

Dad is someone who was there when I had a problem; he listened patiently when I thought I was through with living, and I wanted to give up. He said, "You're not. You're just beginning your life. Things may be difficult right now, but life will get better."

Right after that talk, things got really bad. My dad was accused of a crime he did not commit. Because of this, I was placed in foster care. I still had our talk in my head, remembering the words that were said. My heart was empty without him with me every day. Times would change, and things would get better. The truth was discovered, and my dad's innocence was proven. Therefore, I was allowed to return home, and my dad and I were together again.

We still had talks, but I'm over that hill in my life. Because of my dad and his talks, I am a better person and am growing every day. I love my dad; he is special to me. I'm glad I got to know him.

Dad is someone who is there when I need to laugh or cry. It does not matter what:

I love you, Dad!
Patty, my little sister

When I was born, Daddy was not present. He was out on the road, truck driving. However, when he made it home, we instantly bonded. At two, I would drape a blanket over my shoulders and declare to him, "I'm gonna be a moobie 'tar." As a child, I climbed on his lap, and he would assure to me I was Daddy's girl. Then, at age four on Christmas Day, the unspeakable happened. Daddy had his first major heart attack. Doctors gave him a year. However, he was determined to win, and he began his fight for life.

My dad did his best to be a daddy to five very unique, gifted children. To me, as a fragile girl, he encouraged me to be strong. I think this is why I connected with him in the area of sports. We would play-fight like kickboxing or boxing. At the same time, he brought out my intelligence. We had so many debates over history, politics, and current events! At sixteen, when I gave my heart to Jesus, this became my main topic. I thought I had to win Dad for Christ. Truth is, my dad had a relationship, his relationship, with Christ. At the time of my salvation, Dad was struggling with his faith in Christ, but I witnessed this faith in my dad come to life again. Dad emerged into a godly father and husband.

As a teenager, I began to want to achieve something outside of my family, and I became a worker in school, church, and my community. However, because of a childhood with abuse, my dad's illness, and my family's social status, I was insecure. I developed an eating disorder that would be the beginning of my life with mental illness.

The years before my dad's death, he was the person I could go to who I knew wouldn't judge me, who would love me unconditionally. At the same time, he pushed me.

The quote I will never forget pushes me to this day: "Tif, whatever you do, be good at it! If you are going to be bad or crazy, be good at being bad or crazy. However, if you want to be good, be good at being good."

Daddy

Wrinkles iron face,
your face...
Camouflage the man, the man underneath.
Each line marks a moment.
A moment time has swallowed;
A little boy lost in foster care
only to be sent to war;
returned to the states a man,
a man bound to drugs and beer.
Met wife in an amusement park.
three boys, two girls together.
Heart attack at thirty-seven.
Left sick, vulnerable in a state of depression
Only to live on as inspiration.
Many battle songs you sang to your children,
to me:
Surpassed prognosis.
Over twenty years.
Now, the wheelchair announces,
your wheelchair announces.
you are tired, you need rest.
You tell me not to mourn when you leave.
Oh, Daddy, please stay!

The Day My World Stopped

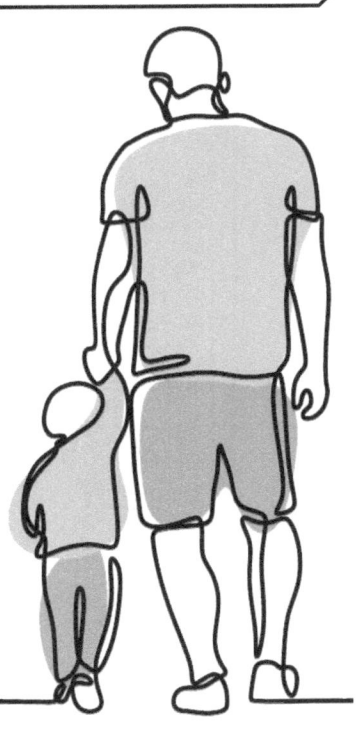

Prologue

Thursday, February 21, 2008, my life was put on hold. On this day, my daddy, Mitchell Francis Burch Sr., died. It is said that there are six stages of grief: shock, denial, anger, depression, bargaining, and acceptance.

Wednesday, February 20, 2008, I, went about my usual schedule. I woke up early for my first class at 8:30 a.m. at the University of Oklahoma in Norman, Oklahoma. It was a sunny, cold winter day. That day I was at the top of my classes. The semester before I was named to the Dean's List, and I became a scholarship finalist for the College of Arts and Sciences. I worked at the Athletic Department at OU and tutored many of the university's finest athletes. I was rising fast, and I was unstoppable; nothing could steal my joy.

Unfortunately, I had caught every flu bug of the season, which weakened my immune system, so I had to visit the health center on campus where I was diagnosed with an ear infection. Because of doctor's orders, I had to stay home from work and classes. This was a much needed rest from the busyness of my hectic schedule. That night I turned off my phones, lounged on my couch, and watched a Disney movie. Then I went to bed early.

Shock: Refuge in Christ

As I slept, images of my dad's death flooded my mind. Then, I saw his face, and the phone rang. It was my sister, and I knew; but a part of me held on to hope. Maybe he will wake up, and he will live once again. I called all my friends, and I requested prayer. I cried and had a hard time keeping a straight head. I forced myself to shower and dress and ride the bus to campus. I was thinking this would be the last shower I would have for a while. Part of me hoped for Daddy to live; the other part knew the truth, and the truth was Daddy was weak and tired.

I stepped off the bus and walked across the street in the center of campus when my cell rang. It was my sister: "He's dead..." My world froze, and I screamed, "No!" As my phone slipped from my fingers, a friend, Edie, walked toward me. Having no idea what was going on, she hugged me as I sobbed uncontrollably. How could I go on?

This cold day in February flashed by in a blur. My friends, Edie and Jackie, surrounded me with love and allowed me to take refuge in their home as I came to grips through a fog of shock.

For two days I hibernated in this home as my friends went about their day-to-day business. My best friend was Sadie, a golden retriever. I cried and hugged that precious dog as I watched movies, and I cried. My friends had Valentine suckers. I kept my energy up by sucking on these calming candies.

It was Friday, February 22, 2008. Jackie hosted a get- together for international students. I forced myself to take a bath and change. I put on a smile as students danced and prepared a fabulous meal. I looked at the happy faces, and I envied them; I wanted to be them. This was the night before I was to return home, and I lost it.

My friends prayed vigorously for me, and I finally fell asleep. I was awakened to my friends inviting me to the living room where my Chi Alpha minister and associate minister and many of my friends were. Never in my life had I received such compassion. Nick and Blake and my beautiful friends spoke words of life to my broken spirit, and to conclude the night, Blake played worship music, and we united in voice. Such an overwhelming peace flooded my soul. This night was so significant. All I could say was, "My daddy would love this; he always said he had hallelujah choirs singing in his ears." Everyone laughed and left. Jackie loaned me her bed, and once again I fell asleep.

During this terrible darkness in my life, I found refuge in the safety of my sisters in Christ.

The Empty Chair

My journey home was cheerful. I rode up with my sister-in-law's dad. It was calm and emotional, but Richard tailored to my needs in that moment. Everyone tried to prepare me for the instant of when I would see the reality that my dad was gone. I had no idea.

It was muddy outside. I remember wiping my shoes on the porch. I exchanged hugs with my mom and sister, and I took a breath as I entered the small, old country house. The kitchen looked like it had two weeks earlier on my brief visit home. It was then I saw the empty chair. The pink, cushiony chair sat empty with the Reese's pillow I had given Daddy two weeks earlier.

I did not know how to respond. I was still in a state of shock. Even through the numbness, I felt a twinge of pain for Daddy. I thought, *Where is he? Is he at peace? What am I going to do without him?*

Denial: Truth in Christ

It would have been so easy to stay in shock, but this does wear off. My reality check occurred the day of my daddy's visitation. The day before, I went to church. It was almost surreal. No one could soothe the pain inside, that is, no one but God. Father God took me in His arms and held me. For a few moments, I was a little girl again lost in the arms of my daddy. The difference for me was that my earthly daddy was in heaven now. My mind could not grasp it.

This is where denial came. When grief sets in, there is a portion of the brain that remains in denial in hopes that it is all a dream. I went to bed at night knowing my daddy was dead, and I would wake up and forget. It was like he died over and over in my mind.

This too faded over time. The following letters, journal entries, poetry, and essays mark my letters to discovery.

Does Death Hurt, Daddy?

8:50 a.m.
Dad
Tick.. .tock.. .the heart
Pounds the chest
A pain burns in the leg
Tick. tock.
Bam!

———•———•———•———

Mom
A smile, a kiss, a joke
Laughter exits
Returns.
A loud thump!

———•———•———•———

Patty
Grinds teeth
In a sweet bliss
House shakes sister awakes.

Jerry
Snores resting
Unaware
A scream!

———————

Tiffany
Daddy enters the dream
His face floats behind the eyelids
The phone sings...

———————

CPR palpitations
Fail to revive
The man, the man inside—

———————

Phone rings!
"He's dead.. .Daddy's dead!"
No!

Sifting through
the Grief

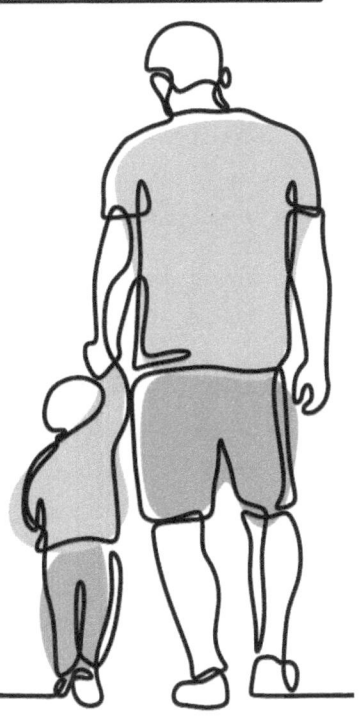

Mom's Letter to Daddy:
'Til Death Do You Part

02-24-08

Dear Mitch,

It's hard to believe that you are not here with me anymore. Each day that passes by takes me further away from the last day I had with you. It happened so fast.. .one minute you were talking to me, and the next minute you were gone. I love you so much. I know that each day that goes by should be easier. But it's going to take time. I know I should be grateful for the days God let you be with us—twenty years longer than the doctor said you would live. You got to see our children grow up to become adults, have kids of their own. Maybe we won't actually be able to see you, but you will always be on our minds and in our hearts forever and ever.

We've been together over thirty-two years. We've almost made it to thirty-three. I knew I'd lose you someday. I knew you were slowly slipping away from us. Your mind and spirit were strong, but your body was getting more and more tired with each passing day. I tried to stay busy and not think about it. I knew you were dying, but you wanted us to be happy, not sad. We've had a lot of years together.. .some good, some bad, but we did the best that we could. We were part of each other—like one person instead of two. You were my best friend! I love you and miss you so much, but I know I have to go on. That's what you would want me to do. It seems like a bad dream. Even though I know it is true, it's going to take a while for reality to sink in. But I know I have to be strong. You'll always be a part of our lives. I can't talk to you in my mind.

Every one of our kids is taking your death hard. It was so sudden. But you'd be proud of them! They are dealing with it in their own ways. You are finally going to get the honor you should have gotten while you were alive. You are going to be buried at Ft. Gibson, Oklahoma. It's a little farther away from all of us than we wanted but not too far away that we all won't be able to visit you. This is just where your body will be. Your spirit will live on and on. Your body was so tired; you will be in your final resting place. Maybe now you will get the rest you need. You won't have to suffer from pain anymore, go to doctors, and take so much medication. Even though it is hard right now, I know I will get through this with God's help.. .one *day* at a time.

You will always be a part of my life no matter what the future holds. We spent every day together that we could since the day we met... had five kids together. I am not saying we were perfect and that it was easy, but we made it with God's help. Most people wouldn't have been able to make it through. Maybe some of the decisions weren't always the right ones, but we did the best that we could. We moved around a lot. You changed jobs a lot when you were able to find work. We had lots of financial problems; who doesn't have problems? Life is no bed of roses. It is full of lots of thorns.

Even though I will always love you, I am glad you are at peace with God. I can see so much of you in our kids and our grandkids. You will never be forgotten. You made a big impact on a lot of lives in your life. We will always miss you, but I know you'd want us all to move forward. You always said you can't change the past. We never know what our future will have in store for us. All we can do is live *one day at a time*! I will always hear your voice and see you in my mind. I know some days are going to be harder than others, but I know I'll make it with God's help.

You take care, and remember we all loved you very much. We will always miss you, but, hopefully, each day will get easier. We all take life for granted. We think that someone we love will be with us forever. It doesn't always work that way. We all have to do the best we can to get through each day. It will be harder for some of us than others. I'll always have a place in my heart for you, and eventually it'll be easier, but right now it is not. I love you and miss you so much. You were the only person in my whole life who I could talk to and not worry about you judging me. I could be myself. You are a lot of the reason I'm as strong of a person as I am today. Sometimes I was okay with having to take care of mostly everything. Other times I wished you could have helped me a little bit more. It was hard at times, but I understood that even though you wanted to, your body wasn't able to cooperate. I'll always love you and miss you very much, but I know even though I don't want to, I have to let you go to be with God. I'm not saying it will be easy, and I won't be angry with God. I will take one day at a time; I have to let you rest in peace. Remember I will always love you, and the years we had together won't be forgotten. You'll always be in my heart and on my mind. Even the little things count!

Your wife of thirty-two-plus years, I'll always love you and miss you, honey!

Your loving wife,
Jeanine

Patty's Early Journal Entries: "Shock"

Thursday, February 21, 2008
Dear Dad,

Today was really bad. We lost you. You were a big part of my life, my daddy for over twenty-three years. I woke up this morning to screams from Mom. She said you are dead. She, Jerry, and the paramedics tried to bring you back, but you were already gone. I called so many people. I was in shock, so was everyone else I called. I miss you, Daddy.

Love,
Patty

Friday, February 22, 2008
Dear Daddy,

Today was as tough as yesterday. People say sorry like they know how I feel; they don't! I am sad and upset. I went to school later. The Kings gave me a Burden Bear; Pam and Johnny gave us food and a card. Corban and Bastian know about you, Dad. Corban is really upset. I love you, Dad!

Love,
Patty

Saturday, February 23, 2008
Dear Daddy,

Today was day number three. It is still hard to deal
with. Tiffany came home from Norman. We watched
The Game Plan. Tif and I talked for a while. The
landlady brought chicken for us. Mitch was here, and
so was Tasha. I love you, Daddy!

Love,
Patty

Sunday, February 24, 2008
Dear Dad,

Today started early. We, Tif and I, went to Sunday
school. We learned a lot. Church was good; our family
was on the prayer list. Marsha was on the prayer team,
and she prayed with us. Kay and Larry came over. I am
surprised very much. Tif was concerned and asked if
I needed to go to the hospital. She played with clay,
and we went to bed. I love you, Daddy!

Love,
Patty

Monday, February 25, 2008
Dear Daddy,

Today was hard. Dad, I saw you sleeping in your casket; it was hard; you looked so peaceful. People came, including some we didn't know. Some people were rude to you at the visitation. We ate at the First Christian Church. A lot of people love you, a lot of flowers. I love you, Daddy!

Love,
Patty

Tuesday, February 26, 2008
Dear Daddy,

Today was rough. We were headed to your funeral and got the wrong exit and went fifty miles out of the way. We got there forty minutes late. The chaplain talked and said how good of a man you were. They gave a flag to Mom. Everyone cried; we miss you badly. I love you, Daddy!

Love,
Patty

"Denial"

Wednesday, February 27, 2008
Dear Daddy,

Today I worked on art. My snowman is coming along. I got thirty dollars for gas so Mom and Tim could take Mitchy to the airport. Things with money are tough. I cried today. How I miss you badly! I love you, Daddy!

Love,
Patty

Thursday, February 28, 2008
Dear Daddy,

Today I went to school early. Toni was sick. I am painting a man with red eyes. French was hard. I am doing well, though. Tonight we went and watched Drake play a clown. Sam and Diane were there. He did well. I love you, Daddy!

Love,
Patty

Friday, February 29, 2008

Today was good. I went to school until ten-ish. We got *Cops* at Grove, which was cool. I took it easy for the rest of the day. Life is getting easier. I love you, Daddy!

Love,
Patty

Friday, March 1, 2008
Dear Daddy,

Today was a good day. I got up earlier and lay around for a while and watched TV, mostly *Cops*, which I love a lot. I know you would too. I miss you a lot. Heather brought Nate over. We played, and she took him home. Fun! He took four steps; I am proud of him. I watched TV for the rest of the night on the couch. We love you, Daddy!

Love always,
Patty

Saturday, March 2, 2008
Dear Daddy,

Today started around eight-ish. I got up and watched TV for a while, *Seventh Heaven*. Aunt Kay texted me earlier, six-ish. I did homework for three hours and still did not get it. I will. Tif got out; she is doing well. *Oprah's Big Give* premiered tonight. Good night! I love you, Daddy!

Love always,
Patty

My Letters to Dad:

April 18, 2008
Dear Daddy:

It has been nearly two months since you died. My life stopped that day. I can see the wrinkles on your face, your shining eyes, and bright smile. When you left, Dad, I had a hard time living on. Past, present, future flooded in, all in one moment. I could not cope. I was on a guilt trip and on my pity pot. I can hear your voice now your lecture. But, Daddy, guess what? I am getting better. They released me early from the hospitals on good behavior. I guess I am no longer good at being crazy. I have to change my agenda and be good at living, my life, a gift. Daddy, OU is working with me. You always said I was blessed with many chances—well, here is to another. I am going to make you proud. I won a scholarship. I can't believe it! God is so awesome! How is Jesus-living working for you? I know it is great to be in heaven. But, Daddy, I wish you were here. We never went fishing, but I will go, and you will just have to be there. I love you, Daddy! I will never forget you! I will carry on as one of your legacies. I will write, smile, live, love, and teach. Oh, and I will keep the faith and look up in all times.

Love,
Tif

April 21, 2008
Dear Daddy,

Hey! What's up? How is heaven treating you? Say "hi!" to Jesus, David, Daniel, Moses, Jeremiah, and the heroes named and unnamed. I bet you're living it up there. We miss you! Mom hides her tears; Patty and I scuffle some, but we are working on straightening up. The guys are trying to be brave. Still, you would be proud. We haven't killed each other. So you died so that you can know all the secrets of the world. And you help put a good word in for KU. Well, if that's what it takes... I love you so much, and I wish you were here! But I will hang in there! Until, I write again.

Love Always,
Tif

April 22, 2008

Hey, Daddy!

What's up? I guess, technically, you are. I miss you so much! My heart aches to see you again. I miss the way you talk, laugh, listen, and smile. Who looked better than you? Daddy, why did you leave us? I know you were tired; life is so different without you here. I look around, and you are gone, absent. I see a photo, but your body is in a casket in the ground in Ft. Gibson National Cemetery. Daddy, how do I hold on without you? You always spoke to me in ways no one else could. Daddy, I was proud to have you as my dad. No dad could have done better. There are things in life I don't understand. But what's in the past is finished! You became a man who all your children could learn from. You inspired anyone you met. We all were proud of you. Thank you for instilling passion, love, and dreams in me. I am blossoming into a woman, a woman with destiny, with purpose, a woman who can pursue anything. I will live as your legacy! I say thank you, Daddy. Say hi to everyone in heaven for me. Don't be too ornery.

Love Always,
Tif

April 25, 2008
Dear Daddy,

As the rain pounds, *pitter patter,* to the ground, my heart stings of all I have lost because of your death. Daddy, I miss our pep talks, your laugh, and the joy of life that you shared to all who would listen. Daddy, there are things I want to understand as well. Why did you have to suffer for someone else's sins? I guess I will take this question to my grave and ask Jesus when we are face-to-face. Daddy, no matter what sins you committed, you became a man I am proud to have known.

Love Always,
Tif

April 29, 2008
Dear Daddy,

The sun shines through the window, and I can only think that you are smiling down from heaven as I soak in the warm rays of sunshine. In the morning, I kiss your picture. I am living, not just existing. Your photo reminds me. I hear your voice: *Tiffany, whatever you do...be good at it.* I tried to be the best at being crazy. But, Daddy, I am no good at it. So, Daddy, I am going to work on being good at living! It is kind of weird. At OU, I have found myself. I am blossoming into the young woman I was meant to be. I am full of life— passion, zeal, ambition—all kindle to fire up living. I, Tiffany Dawn Burch, am going to take risks, to stand up, and be proud of who I am. No longer will I retreat; no longer will I be defeated. God has a perfect plan for me. I will stand up and fight. Daddy, I will adhere to your example. You never stopped fighting to the end. Daddy, I am proud of what you had grown to be. I hope I can live on as your legacy.

Love always,
Tif

April 30, 2008
Dear Daddy,

Another day has passed, and your absence is heavily felt. But, Daddy, I am remembering your pep talks, and I am actually doing what you said. I feel so much peace inside. I can do this; I can live, not just exist. Recovery is not easy; I know you remember your journey. I hold your AA book, and I am reading it. I may not be an alcoholic, but I am an addict. Until I own up to it, I will struggle. Doctors labeled me hopeless, but I am not. I am a girl, a spoiled girl, with an addiction, one that has left me powerless. Daddy, I thank you for leading me to this revelation. Say hi to everyone in heaven for me. Now you get to be a part of the hallelujah choir you had always heard in your head. I will always love you and keep you close to my heart.

Love,
Tif

May 27, 2008
Dear Daddy,

I know I have shut down for a month. I guess I have reached some sort of acceptance of your death for the most part. However, the first week of May I struggled, for my birthday was to follow. I felt a void; you have always been a part of that special day for me, and I dreaded your absence. To not hear your "Happy Birthday" sung in off key was more than I could bear. I cried a lot, almost every day. And then, the storm inside calmed, and I held on. Daddy, I held on to God; I knelt at the throne of Jesus, and I laid down my pain. I still cried, but the pain is becoming less. And my birthday, wow! I embraced the moment, presents, and cake. (I ate your slices.) I also have made some personal absolutions. This is still not easy. I know what you'd say concerning the Linda dilemma, but I know now the truth, and the good book says the truth shall set you free. I love you! I can never forget you. Daddy, if you could only see your family now; I am sure you have front row seating in heaven, so I know you are proud of what we have done since you left. I am just sad that it took you dying to bring me home and make me come to my senses and let go of my drama-queen act. Guess what! I like myself, and I am loving this life. I am painting, sculpting, doing chores, and embracing the simplicity of country life, yet I see the beauty in the synchronization of country life. Again, say hi to everyone for me.

Love always,
Tif

June 1, 2008

Hola, Daddy! Yet another month started without my daddy; how I miss you! You think with this much time, over three months, that it would be easier to cope with, but with each day that passes, your loss is more real. Between your lectures and laughs, how are we going to make it without you, Daddy? I wish I could rewind time; I wish I could hug you one more time, give you one more kiss, and see you alive one more moment. Well, Daddy, enough pitying my own emotions. You will never leave my heart!

Love Always,
Tif

June 19, 2008
Dear Daddy,

Sixteen weeks, incredible! It really has been a long sixteen weeks. You know that is the length of a semester. Wow! How time slips away. Mom, Sis, and I visited your resting place Sunday on Father's Day. Officially, it was our first one without you. Daddy, that word does not add justice to your name. Daddy, why did we take you for granted? Your farewell kisses I have never forgotten. I wish I could have one more moment with you here on earth, but Daddy, your family will meet you in heaven. I guess you had to go pick our house in heaven. Between the hallelujah choir, old timers, Jesus, and unlimited fishing time, I know you are being fulfilled. No more sickness, sadness, lies. You are free, Daddy. I hope I can live my life just as free. Daddy, you told me to look up and trust God, not man. If I only knew what you meant when you were here. I guess that is the beauty of life. Daddy, I am becoming a woman. I am not crazy, but you already knew that. I can hear your laughs from heaven. By the way, I am going back to OU, but you already knew that as well.

Love always,
Tif

June 24, 2008
Dear Daddy,

Hey! I miss you so much. How my heart aches to see you, hear your voice, and hug you. I am trusting God so much more, though. When my emotions become intense, I look up and smile. God is in control! Then, peace floods my soul. Surrendering is a technique I am trying to master. You were such a pro. We all have our quarks, so God is teaching me a new thing called faith. I hope that life is in God's hands. Daddy, my heart aches for Mom. She misses you. She tries to hide her tears, but the love you shared is evident. I know this is part of the grief process, but if you could put in a good word for her, Daddy, she needs some major blessings poured out on her life—her life she sacrificed for you and her children...need I say more? Patty has done a 180-degree turn. She is growing into an amazing woman, but she is still Sis. She will never stop being Patty, and I am learning as much from her as she is from me. Four months, sixteen-plus weeks, and two seasons have passed. Your death is no easier today than it was then; your absence is felt deeply by all of us. The cool thing is we will meet you in heaven. Daddy, your baby girl will rock this world and live. Until we meet again. I love you and carry you close to my heart.

Love always,
Tif

June 30, 2008
Dear Daddy,

I guess you have been talking to Jesus and putting in good words for your beautiful family. Peace is liquid here. We all connect on different levels we could have only dreamed of in days past. Mom, she smiles, teases, and laughs. Today, I held the Serenity Prayer bookmark she received for her eight-grade graduation. I had no idea at the moment, but tears flowed down my face. I thought of you, and I cried more. Mom looked at me, and I held it up and gave it to her. She handed it back and said I could keep it. It was a connection I never expected, but it was like layers of walls were instantly torn down. God's love is amazing! I bet heaven is treating you nicely. How we miss you here! Patty and I were thinking the other day about when you took her, Tim, and me to the strip pits to fish in Kansas. I guess I got to go fishing with you after all. When I feel down, I think of you, which makes me look up, so I do and smile. I sing praises and become free. The Lord is amazing! Thank you, Daddy, for all the wonderful happy memories you left to us, your family, to me, your oldest daughter. I love you, Daddy! I hold you close to my heart.

Love always,
Tif

July 17, 2008
Dear Daddy,

Nearly a month has passed since my last entry. I have been unable to put pen to paper. Until July 4, my life was flowing like water in a creek. Then a rock came and smacked me in the face on July 4. Heather, in anger, threw daggers like fire at me with her tongue. The sting is more than I could show. I cannot see my precious nephews and niece, which is hard, but you did not raise me up to be a wimp. I took it like a woman. Then the next day, Teah, the family dog, died in my arms. Daddy, I couldn't save her. She died. I tried to help her. I cleaned the building and gave the dogs food and water. I thought she was hot, so I hosed her down. I had no idea she would die. I know what you would say, so I looked up to God, and I realize some things in my life are out of my control. I am going back to OU to finish what I started. I went through "Mama's Boot Camp," and I have lasted longer than any other program I have been through. I am so glad to be alive. Not that I don't have moments. Somehow I remember you and Mom and the life of survival of love, laughter, and dreams you instilled in me. With commitment, a little endurance, I will go far, so watch me, Daddy, from your big TV in the sky. Until we meet again, I will carry you close to my heart.

Love always,
Tif

July 31, 2008
Hey, Daddy!

How my heart longs to hear you; your voice echoes from my mind to my ears. Oh, Dad! We visited you Monday on your fifty-ninth birthday. I have been unable to write the pain my heart had felt; your absence is deeply felt by us all. We swap stories, hoping somehow we can bring you alive through our memories. I know, Daddy, you are alive in heaven, so I hold on to hope that one day we will be reunited. Your grandkids miss their papa, but being young, they do not know how to express it. I know for sure they will never forget you. Your legacy flows through all our veins. And, Daddy, when I marry and have children, I will share you with them. They will know of the man who raised me, the man who I know as Daddy. I start OU this next month. I have won another chance; maybe life won't be so dramatic for me this semester. I don't want to be bored, but I want to be successful. I want to make friends and finish what I have started. As you watch your big TV and fish and sing in the hallelujah choir, please put in a good word for me and this family. Daddy, I will always carry you close to my heart.

Love always,
Tif

August 9, 2008
Dear Daddy,

How my heart aches. Today, a family day yet not even close. I keep expecting to hear your voice, to hear you telling your children to cut the crap, but all I hear is silence. We move like nothing happened. I am trying to grow up, Daddy! I have been less than perfect, and I have screwed up more times than I can count. Haven't we all? I want Tim and Heather to understand; I love them. I just want forgiveness. Even though Heather publicly humiliated me and is keeping my nephews and niece away, I forgive her. Even though Tim has denied me the chance to even tell him what happened, I forgive him. I forgive them even though the sting is unbearable. Yet on the upside, I am not running away; I am not avoiding; I am writing letters. Maybe somehow they can find it in their hearts to forgive, let go, and move on. If not, it is not my burden to bear. If God forgives me, that is all that matters. Daddy, thank you for your forgiveness. I hated myself for what I said and thought about you. Thank you for seeing through all that and knowing I truly love you, and I totally had an identity crisis, but you never held it against me. Thank you! I can let go, I can move on, I can, and I will! I miss you so I am blowing kisses to you from earth to your palace in heaven. Until we meet again, enjoy your vacation in paradise, if God does not keep you too busy. Know I keep you close to my heart!

Love always,
Tif

The Six-Month Mark...

Sunday, August 3, 2008:

A Summer in the Middle of Nowhere

How could I know that a summer with my family could help me find me, Tiffany? For so long, I have run away from who I really am. I rushed and rushed. Things kept happening, including a flood last summer and the death of my daddy last February. I thought if I kept going, if I did not stop and take a breath that I would be okay. Then I just burned out. After Dad died, I tried to continue on with classes. A few days after I returned, I got really sick and had to go to the hospital where I stopped breathing. I was put on a ventilator. When I woke up, I forgot everything I learned that semester, and I was unable to fulfill my duties as a tutor. On top of that, I was accused of self-inflicting this. It hurt, and under the pressure, I snapped. I had to be hospitalized on a psyche ward to begin the process of grieving. But God has a way of remedying all situations. At first, my journey home was tough; my mom has lived out in the middle of nowhere, and I kind of like college life in Norman. Plus, I have a younger sis who I thought would drive me crazy. Then, I realized how awesome country life was for the healing and grieving process. Patty and I worked through our differences; we both began to lean on each other and develop our relationships with Jesus.

I got to see my family in a whole different light. Mom and I spent much time together, especially in the beginning when I was struggling with the intense pain of losing my dad, talking about God and heaven and our relationship with God. It has been awesome, and my brother, Jerry, and I connected in some ways. Dad's death did a lot of things in my family; it brought us closer together, and it helped us all become closer to God.

Well, so many things happened to me in my personal walk with Jesus. A lot of things I learned from OU Chi Alpha Latenight, Lifegroups, Elevate, SALT, and others I was able to put to practice. I have kept an active devotion and prayer life. This has been the key ingredient to moving beyond my pain. I mixed this with lots of praise and worship time, and I have kept up with many journals. In all these things, I have found peace.

Outside of all this, I have kept up with hobbies; I was amazed at what one can do if they take the time. I made lots of things with my hands, including a lighthouse and many pieces of jewelry. Exercise became another thing I have had to do. I walked my dog(s) daily and took nature walks with my sis, Patty. Since it has become really hot, I have had to exercise inside. Being in the country, I think I hit my all-time record in watching movies, but this too has been fun.

I still miss being in civilization around other human being but being able to stay home has been somewhat of a miracle for me, and I will never trade my summer for anything. Isn't God good?

Dad's Letter to Me

January 2000
Dear Tif,

How are you doing today? I hope fine. I love and miss
you girls a lot. You two are more important to your
mother and me than anything. We haven't forgotten
about you all; we feel you all need more time to get
things sorted out. I just want you to get well. I know
it is hard for you all, but hang in there and do what
they tell you. Tif, I forgive you, but you have to forgive
yourself. You can't live on a guilt trip. I am feeling
fine right now. I think I will wait to go to church. I
like your church but feel bad about what's happened.
I thought I would write you a line and let you know
I still love you.

Love you!
Dad

Reflections: The Journey through Grief, How God Led me to Freedom!

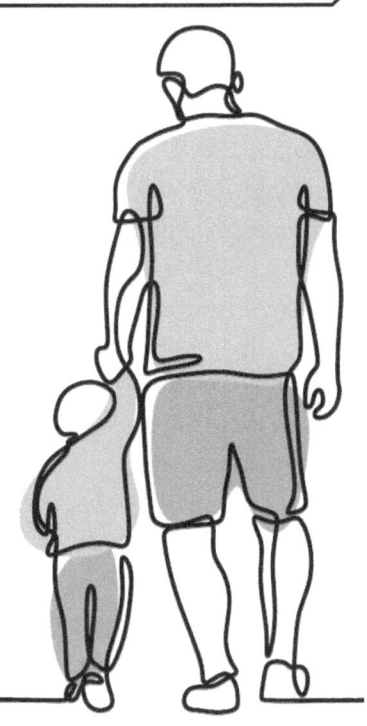

February 2, 2012

When I think back four years ago to the day my daddy died, I am in awe of how God led me from the depths of despair to the woman of God I am today. The road has been long, and I have found myself in a lot of dark places, but along the way my Father in heaven never left me, nor did He forsake me.

Denial to Anger to Depression:

In the fall of 2008, I returned to OU with all the promise and hopes it had for me. This time was different because I took a special person with me, my little sister, Patty. By this time, I had worked through denial and the letters to my dad stopped, but nothing could prepare me for the anger that captured my being. I was angry that my dad died. I was angry that not only two weeks after my dad died, I ended up in an unexplained coma, and when I woke up, I lost everything I worked so hard to gain. I was angry that Teah, our beloved family dog, died in my arms, and I could do nothing to save her. I was angry that my brother would not speak to me and that his wife hated me because I confided a family secret in a friend who told Heather. Heather and Tim's refusal to forgive me shocked my family, who was already grieving my dad's death. A close family became fragmented.

The event happened on a very difficult day for the family, July 4, 2008, our first Independence Day without Dad. Mom, Patty, and I picked up my youngest nephew, Nathan, at my brother's house for a family celebration. We went and had a great time. I thought my family was okay; I had no idea what was about to come. When we returned to drop off Nathan, Heather was angry. She started screaming that Tim should have dealt with me three months ago when I returned home. The words sunk in my bleeding heart like a dagger. That day I had to deal with the loss of my dad, my brother, my nephews, my niece, and any hope of a relationship with my sister-in-law. With this event, Heather refused to let me be an aunt to my nephews and niece, and Tim refused to acknowledge me. I could not understand, because even through Heather's hate, I loved her.

However, even with all this against me, I marched forward to my dream at OU, excited for a clean slate and a new semester to attack and achieve on my way to the finish line of graduation. Unfortunately, nothing was the same! My friends, who once were close to me, began to repel from me. I did not understand, for at this time I was socially awkward, and I maintained very few long-term friendships.

Then, the demands of OU began to take its toll on my sister and me. We both ended up inpatient in hospitals for different reasons. This sent red flags up to all who knew us, and we were banned from a Christian event. I understand how it looked to those involved, but what they did not understand, what they could not see was beyond what was going on, how my heart needed seeds of love more than ever.

I was dying on the inside more and more every day. Don't get me wrong; I loved God, but the anger became a toxin that poisoned me from the inside. And the more that the devil could make me see how worthless I was, the more I wanted to escape from the living hell that I walked in.

I was no longer at the top of my classes. I struggled to even make it to classes. Before the coma, I saw the world in black and white. When I awoke I saw the world in color. While this became a good thing, in the beginning it was a shock to my brain. Nothing in Norman was the same as it had been before. Out in the country at Mama's Boot Camp, I was sheltered in a cocoon. However, the real world can be cruel and lonely. Without God, it can become impossible to hold on, and for me, it almost was.

With each day that passed, the grief and anger that flooded my soul began to take its toll on every aspect of my life to the point I felt suffocated, and I knew I could not manage in Norman, so I reached out to a woman I thought could help me. I called her, and she agreed to let me come stay and work out my issues in her residential treatment program. This person tried to help me, but she was not God and could not be His substitute. I am sure she did not realize how fragile I was in that moment.

This woman decided to travel with me to help me pack my belongings in Norman and return to her place where I would begin a program to help me overcome my issues. However, this did not happen as we planned it.

We drove a total of eight hours in two days, and I did most of the driving. Anger began to mix with anxiety, and not even a mile from her place, she asked me to brighten the lights. The vehicle was unfamiliar to me, so I was not quick enough. She said never mind, but I finally figured it out, and she went ballistic on me. She thought I was being smart aleck about it, and maybe I was, but I was emotionally exhausted, and the last thing I needed was that. Looking back, I know she was tired too, but in the moment, it was like the last bit of poison ready to destroy a dying soul.

She demanded that I get out of the vehicle and let her drive. At that moment, I made a decision to end my life. I did not care anymore! I was through with trying! I wanted the pain to stop!

Hell Is Real!

I walked the last mile back to the country house. I was given a small room in a trailer, and I already in my mind had it planned. I grabbed the pills, all of them, and I swallowed all that I could. Then, being high on adrenaline, I began to walk on the country dirt road. Within minutes, I began to feel the effects of the drugs. The world began to spin, but somehow by the grace of God in the dark in the middle of nowhere, I made it to a home of a woman and her family who was able to call an ambulance.

In the time it took for help to get there, I knew I was dying physically. It was hard to breathe, and my body was on fire. I could feel death trying to suck me away, and I could see snakes slithering around me, ready to seep their venom in my veins. The help finally arrived. Unfortunately, by the time they arrived, I was already slipping away to a place I will never forget.

I remember the sensation of fire burning my skin and how I struggled to capture my breath; just when I thought it was over and that I could breathe again, the fight to breathe would continue. The pain was like thousands upon thousands of needles piercing my skin. I remember the high shrill of screams that were worse than any horror movie I had ever watched; the fumes of death worse than the smell of skunk and rotten eggs combined entered my nostrils. All I wanted was a taste of water to alleviate my thirst.

As if this was not enough, these beings that I believe to be demons began to taunt me. They laughed at me, prodded me, saying over and over and over that I got what I deserved. I tried to tune it out, but their attacks became more vicious, and nothing I did prevented me from feeling or seeing what was happening. I am not sure when I realized what was happening or where I was! I kept thinking, *this has to be a bad dream!* However, I knew that all my five senses were not active in my dreams. This was hell! I knew hell was real, but I did not know that my soul was in jeopardy of going there.

You see, down deep inside, I loved Jesus, and I believed in Him. Unfortunately, the truth is in my anger, I began to rebel against God, and my once-on-fire heart became cold. No longer was God my first love! In my anger, I walked away from the values I held dear, and I stopped caring until that dark night in November 2008 when my heart physically stopped and I had a brief encounter with hell. Two days later, I awoke from a coma on a ventilator. I am so thankful to this very day that God snatched me from the pits of hell and gave this wretched soul another chance.

A Dirt-Covered Penny

Rising up from the ashes did not come easy for me. God had to get it through my thick skull that He loved me and wanted me to cast all my cares upon Him. I had to surrender and put my trust in Him. I became a dirt-covered penny trying to discover where I belonged, waiting for the blood of Jesus to cleanse me from my sin and make this penny shine bright again.

A year had passed since my dad's death, and my eyes began to open into how sick my spiritual condition was. In early of March 2009, I found myself in another dark place in sin. I was ready to die, but God saved me again, and I knew I had to repent, turn away from my sin, and return to the foundations that I learned when I met Jesus four days before my sixteenth birthday. That same month I returned home to my mom's, and I found myself back in church.

My first Sunday back at home, the pastor preached about faith, and he asked if anyone needed salvation or needed to return to their salvation from a backslidden condition. I raised my hand, and I recommitted myself to the hands of a loving heavenly Father. I had no idea of the trial and tribulations that were ahead of me; I just longed to be in the presence of my almighty God! For five months, I experienced peace like I had not experienced in over a year. I even got a new apartment and began to adjust to my new life.

Then, bam! Out of nowhere the enemy began to target me. They say when it rains, it pours! Well, in the summer of 2009, this statement rang true. I became sick from mold exposure, and my computer crashed when I had just started an online class. Then, a neighbor began to stalk my sister and me. Being a fiery baby in Christ, I began to seek ways to enrich the kingdom of God. I visited some elderly church members, made gifts for friends, and offered a listening ear to those who needed to talk. I became a sister to our neighbor upstairs, a seventeen-year-old boy who had a rough relationship with his family. One day I went for a walk, and another neighbor was walking his white dog.

He stopped me, so I petted the dog and listened to his tale not knowing that this event would lead him to think I was his girlfriend. One day this man knocked on our door. I opened, and he pushed himself in our apartment. Finally, my sister and I were able to get him to leave. Later that same night, this man broke into the apartment upstairs.

We were terrified, and it got worse. The man would bang on our windows at night, peeping in the windows. The police could not help us because every time they came on scene, he disappeared. My sister coped with the fear by sleeping; I coped with the fear by standing guard, which made me physically and emotionally exhausted. I knew that I had to do something, or this situation would not be resolved.

The Sweet Taste of Freedom

That same summer of 2009, I packed a suitcase, a bag, a purse, and a computer bag to leave behind all I knew to embark on a journey, a journey to something my heart longed for but could not find: *freedom!*

I was angry and alone. I did know Jesus, and I loved Him with all that was in me. However, sometimes the fire is turned up, and things are beyond our control. I had no family or friends to meet me at my point of need. Many tried in ways they could, but the situation with the man that was stalking my sister and me was hot and crazy. I am sure as chaotic as that summer was, it seemed like I lost my mind. I had no support from family or friends, and I felt so alone in the drama that was unfolding. But God! You see, when we are at the end of what we can do, Jesus has the answer.

I could no longer live in my apartment because of this man who was disillusioned to believe that I was his girlfriend to the point he stalked my sister and me. My family forsook me, and the few friends I had did not know what to do or say. I was sleeping under trees here and there, and I was terrified for my sister's life, for my own. Then one night I had enough of the craziness, and I was escorted out of town by two men from our sheriff's department who took me to the state line where another deputy picked me up and took me to a homeless shelter.

I was ready for my life to be over with. I was weak, tired, and I lost everything that ever mattered to me. I was desperate and alone. I was at the end of me. I formed a plan in my head; it would have worked this time. I knew it was selfish, but at that moment, I did not care. I cried out loud, "God, if you want me to not do this, get me out of this somehow!"

I was five yards from my destination when a woman pulled over and asked if I needed a ride. For some reason, I accepted. Even in the pits of despair, I longed for a solution, some hope to this anguish eating me alive. She started talking. She asked me my name; I told her. I do not remember her name. The only thing I remember about this woman is this: she had a daughter named Tiffany. She spoke of her daughter and her granddaughters, and I just knew I could not go through with my plan.

God answered me, and He sent me a mother for a very difficult moment in my life.

I knew I had to live on! As horrible as my life seemed, I had this hope that it would get better. It was the next day that my ticket to my new life, to freedom was purchased. On July 30, 2009, I walked on a Greyhound bus in Joplin, Missouri, to carry me to my new life in McAlester, Oklahoma.

Angry, bound up, tired, I entered a domestic violence shelter. These people loved me despite me. It was there that I was introduced to New Beginnings Church; it was there I was given a chance to breathe, unwind, and find out what this girl named Tiffany Dawn Burch was about.

I am not saying the picture was pretty, or that the journey to freedom was smooth. Far from it! The domestic violence shelter was just the beginning. I had to come to a point where I was prepared to challenge the labels the world put on me and accept the new life God had for me. If you knew me then, you would not even think I was the same girl.

On January 2, 2010, we had a guest speaker at my church, and he gave an altar call. He asked me what I wanted. All I could say was one word: *freedom!* He looked at me, and with a huge smile, he said, "Freedom is going to taste so sweet!"

You know, I had faith for freedom, but what I did not understand and what at that moment I could not comprehend was that freedom for me was going to be a process. And it has been! Piece by piece, the Holy Spirit has cleaned me up and demolished wall after wall that has guarded my heart. There were moments that I even wrestled with God in what He was saying and what He wanted to do, but in the end of the struggle, God got through my thick skull.

God knew what He was doing when He brought me to McAlester, Oklahoma. He put me in a church that took me in as messed up and broken as I was and loved me. New Beginnings Church became my family, and I inherited many sisters in Christ who became my guides and mentors to a new life. I began to create happy memories, and my heart began to melt as I began to trust again.

I would love to say that it was all uphill, but it has not been. I have hit many valleys and struggled through many storms, but the one thing I know is this: God has never left me, nor has He forsaken me! In every storm, on every mountaintop, in every valley, in every victory, in the hog pit, in every moment I stood at death's doorsteps, God has been with me.

Today, I have a life that is better than I used to dream of. I have a normal life away from institutions and hospitals and off the streets. I am not bound to the labels of mental illness or victim or disability. I am not forced to swallow medications to function. My mind is clear; my body is healthy. I have an apartment, my own bedroom, a bed, a closet, air conditioner—things we often take for granted. I am able to give back through volunteer work, the Regina Project (a women's ministry for life after crisis), my church choir, and whatever opportunity God gives me in my neighborhood with my friends or my community. My future is bright! Today, I know this truth that no matter what happens, the good and the bad: Tiffany means to be free! And freedom tastes sweet!

Freedom's Journey

By Tiffany Dawn Burch

Freedom, my heart sings.
In my head a melody rings.
My eyes behold a face in the mirror.
Down my cheek runs a silent tear.
Who is that girl looking back at me?
She is beautiful, glowing, so free
Is that girl in the mirror really me?

Trials and tribulations, the waters and fires
Once consumed my life, my dreams, my desires.
My gifts were tucked away on a shelf in a dark closet
Waiting to be opened in a perfect God designed moment.
My voice was locked inside my heart
Waiting for God to say start!

The process to freedom was not easy for me.
I longed for peace, water for my journey.
The wilderness was dark, cold, and often lonely
And the desert was a dry, heated, land of misery.
Sometimes I searched here and there
For the perfect solution, the perfect answer!

However, I did not find it here or there.
The world had nothing to share.
Instead, the world sucked the life from my soul;
My joy, faith, and hope it stole.
Then, I met Jesus who grabbed my hand
And promised to lead me to a greater land!

When I left behind all I knew,
I had no idea, or even a clue
Of what God was going to do!
Damaged goods, labeled to be thrown away;
God stepped in to show me the way:
How to live, to act, to speak, to pray.

Freedom did not come cheap, nor was it easy;
Why did I expect it to be?
Jesus, sinless, died on the cross for me, so that I could be free!
It was hard for Him, but He did it for me, so that I could be free!
In looking at my journey,
I must remember that it was just that, a journey.

The journey was long, the journey was rough,
But Father God sent me His love!
And today freedom found its way to my soul,
Replenishing the peace, the joy that the devil stole.
His waters are fresh; His waters taste sweet!
I have stepped in, surrendered, and allowed Jesus to defeat!

Thank You, Lord!

This poem captures the story of how I traveled from the depths of despair to freedom. From my teen years to this time of grief, I struggled with an eating disorder. At seventeen I was treated for Bulimia Nervosa. While I quit purging, I continued to binge eat. The grief of losing my dad added to this desire to consume and overindulge in food.

In November of 2010, over two years after my daddy died, my dad's sister died. My aunt could have prolonged her life had she lost weight. However, around the time she died, she lost her ability to move freely. In time, her heart got weaker and stopped. She was only forty-eight years old.

With my dad and aunt's premature deaths and knowing my family history, the reality of my eating problem sunk in. I realized I needed to make changes and to let no more excuses send me to an early grave. I started my weight loss journey at 270 pounds. First, I removed all foods that would sabotage my success. Then, I created a game plan to relearn how to eat and develop an exercise routine. I also had to fight the desire to overeat, which was a coping mechanism that was hard to let go.

Along the way I had to set small goals to reach the big weight loss. With each milestone I hit, I found new ways to boost my motivation, including training for and running my first 5k in April of 2011. I also celebrated each success with a new hairstyle, new outfit, or fun time with some friends. As I lost more weight, most of my motivation to lose weight and be healthy came from an inward drive to change my eating habits and increase my exercise routine.

Reaching the goal to weigh under two hundred pounds was one of the toughest journeys ever. Mostly, I had to learn to accept the woman inside and grow confident in the person I was becoming. I had to learn to cope with emotions, to trust others, and to let others love and support me. I have had to learn to balance nutrition, exercise, and all areas of my life.

Working through an eating disorder is not easy, especially when grief is in the picture. The thing is that I learned to place my bondage in Jesus's hands, and He broke those chains that kept me in a prison. Yes, the enemy has tried to sneak in and remind me of all my imperfections. I have had to learn to love me for who God created me to be. I am a masterpiece in God's eyes created for His glory. I also had to learn that while losing weight is important for health reasons, it is not the most important thing. Balance has become a key principle in my life and has helped me overcome the obsession with food, my body, and my weight.

The Days of
Acceptance

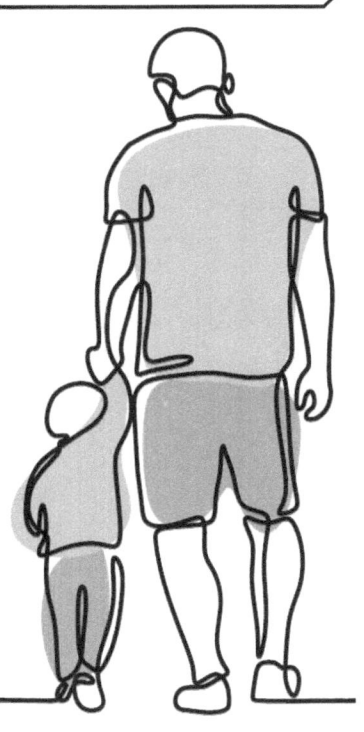

The Man I Knew as Daddy...

The man I knew as Daddy
I met two weeks after my birth.
He was never the average person alive;
His whole life he had to fight to survive.
He stood for justice, love, and freedom No matter what it cost him.
As a young child living in horrible conditions,
He worked hard to take care of the other children,
To protect his mom from danger he was too young to understand.

Foster homes should have been his ticket.
No! More battles to survive he was forced to live.
However, at the age of eighteen, he decided to give
His life for a greater cause.
This country, America, the beautiful, America...
My daddy laid down his life, gave up his dreams for a greater cause
We take for granted:
Freedom!

When he returned home, you would think that he earned his own freedom...
No!
Spit on, mocked, cursed, America he fought for returned her favor
Through many unkind words, deeds, rejection.

In June of 1975,
In an amusement park as a carnival worker,
He met my mom, who became his wife
On July 4, 1975.
Five unique, gifted children they raised together.
Daddy worked hard to keep his family fed;
From an early age, his children he worked hard to equip
With skills they needed to live!
I am not saying my daddy did everything right,
But I am saying he tried with all his might.

Even though my daddy sweated day in and day out, he made time,
He made time for each of us!
However, one cold Christmas day
My daddy had his first heart attack,
And the world we as a family knew was stripped apart.

My daddy was humbled in ways I will never understand;
For many years I did not know the man.
What I do know is this, when I needed him,
He was there!

• • •

Daddy prayed every night for his children
And lived on as an inspiration.
Many battle songs he gave us,
And dreams he allowed us to believe
In hopes we would be free,
free to live, to laugh, to love,
to fight with passion and a purpose from God above.

• • •

Five gifted very individual kids Dad and Mom raised together
Through the good and the bad, they stuck together!
Yes, many times were hard, but there were just as many that were good.
There was a priceless love, money cannot buy that kept us together glued.

• • •

I miss the man I knew as Daddy;
I always will!
But what helps this heart to heal
Is the truth that lives, the truth that is real
That one day despite what I feel
We will be together again in heaven
Free! Free! 100 percent completely free
With no burdens or sin,
No more sorrow or tears!
So, onward I march and move forward in Christ;
to fulfill my purpose destiny in life!
Time to close this chapter, write the next
As I surrender to a greater cause...
To be a sweet vessel to carry the message, love of Jesus
To a world, a world in need,
A world that needs Jesus to be freed.

Thank You, Lord!

Rock of Grief Rolled Away:

I cannot tell you the day it happened, the day that overwhelming rock of grief on my heart was rolled way. What I can tell you is that today my heart has been released from that heavy burden. I would be lying if I say I do not miss Daddy. I still get tears in my eyes when I see his pictures or think of him, especially the important holidays. However, the difference for me today and four year ago is this: I have found a peace in Jesus that is unshakeable! I know that one day I will be reunited with Daddy in heaven. That hope has never left me.

Today, I live on as I pursue a greater calling than myself. No longer do I sit on the sidelines and watch others as I dream of all I can do. God has answered the desires of my heart and has surpassed my wildest imaginations. Today, I am living my dreams, and God has opened the doors for me to bless others time and time again.

Spiritual Family

It has been a wild ride for me as I have waded through the sorrow of grief. Along the way, I inherited a beautiful spiritual family, including a pastor, spiritual mom and dad, and many spiritual sisters and brothers who have lifted me up, encouraged me, and loved me even when I was unable to love back. The best thing about this spiritual family is that they never gave up on me even when it looked hopeless.

So I say to you who are grieving today; plug yourself in a church family today! You cannot go through this journey alone. I, myself, struggled with opening my heart to others. I was broken, scared, and angry; I had been rejected, betrayed, and forgotten. The world gave up on me, but God never did! And He used many people to reach out to me.

In my journey, I have had to remember that people are human and are not a substitute for God. Also, I had to recognize and accept that people do make mistakes. Looking back, I know I have personally made countless mistakes, and I praise God that He has forgiven me! God has cleansed me from head to toe of all the filthiness that once covered me, and He continues to clean my feet when I step in a mess. With the same grace I have been forgiven, I had to learn to forgive others. This shattered the walls that guarded my heart, and I was able to let others in. I will never regret my choice to forgive!

My Heavenly Father

More important than anything I have ever done was my decision to come to my heavenly Father, God. I had to surrender and humble myself before Him. I could not overcome the burden of grief on my own. Once I released the bonds of the burden and accepted God's truth found in the Word of God, I became free!

There is a peace knowing that even though my earthly father has died and gone to heaven, I still have a heavenly Father who is here with me always inside my heart. The joy of the Lord has been and continues to be my strength! The death of my daddy was just one of many life events I have had to face and will face. Even so, I know that no matter what comes my way that my heavenly Father will hold my hand and lead me through the valleys, calm the storms, and cheer me in victory as I stand on the mountain tops.

Hope for the Future

My hope is that everyone who reads this book will hear the heart of my journey and that this will lead them to a greater truth into the arms of a loving heavenly Father who wants to roll the rock of grief away. My prayer is that those who are hurting will find the peace, love, and joy I have discovered in Christ. If God can do it for me, I know He can do it for anyone.

I will extol You, O Lord, for You have lifted me up, and have not let my foes rejoice over me. O Lord my God, I cried out to You, and You healed me. O Lord, You brought my soul up from the grave; You have kept me alive, that I should not go down to the pit. Sing praise to the Lord, You saints of His, And give thanks at the remembrance of His holy name. For His anger is but for a moment, His favor is for life; weeping may endure for a night, but joy comes in the morning.

Psalm 30:1-5 (NKJV)